"Cynthia Burton crafts the divine romance in language that is specially tailored for women. As you walk this guided tour, your heart will burn with fresh desire for Jesus and your soul will recline in the bosom of your Heavenly Father. Embark on the romantic adventure!"
--Bob Sorge, author, SECRETS OF THE SECRET PLACE

"Do you remember your first date? Were you expecting to fall madly in love on that date? It takes time being together for love to grow. The King of Kings seriously pursues you. Cynthia's presentation of special thoughts and words will challenge you to love and be loved. You will grow sure of His pursuit and fall deeper in love. You too can have a meaningful happy forever after knowing you are loved. Are you ready to be loved deeper than you've ever known?"
--Linda Livengood, pastor's wife (10 years), serving as an itinerant evangelist with her husband, Michael Livengood (33 plus years), musician, intercessor, author of self-published Prayer Manuals, and live stream prayer meetings on Periscope/Pray the Word.

"*Date Night with Jesus* is a powerful handbook for experiencing a new depth of relationship, not only with Jesus but with Father God and the Holy Spirit. Each date is a pathway that leads to a compelling desire to walk with The Lord every day. This book is filled with tender love yet straight talk about walking in covenant commitment with the Lord. I love how Cynthia uses God's Word to guide each precious step to a new depth of intimacy with the Lord. I highly recommend *Date Night with Jesus* - You will never be the same after encountering Jesus through your dates with Him."

--Linda Lee, author of Walk with Me - Nuggets of Inspiration, a 30-day devotional.

"Cynthia D. Burton takes a devotional time with Jesus to a whole new level in *Date Night with Jesus*. We have all considered thoughts like an intimate time with Jesus, but Cynthia gives us a practical plan to accomplish that very personal time. The Scripture support of each "date" validates the Father's desire to spend time with us. My highlight of each chapter is the letter at the end. I believe Cynthia stepped into the prophetic to speak the Words of the Father. I could hear Him speaking to me in a way only He can. Having known Cynthia for many years, her ministry and personal relationship with Jesus is a testimony of her practical, intimate relationship with Jesus. Her desire to see others experience Christ on a very personal growing level is evident. I have watched Cynthia grow into a mighty woman of God, and throughout her book, she shares experiences that have led to that growth. Every woman can relate to Cynthia's journey, and we learn that Jesus still loves us in our imperfection, cares more than we can imagine and wants us to have a *Date Night with Jesus!*"

--Kathy Holdeman, Indiana District Women's Director, Assemblies of God

"Intimacy with the Father is what the Lord desires most from His people. We were created to have a relationship with Him. Many do not know or understand how to achieve an intimate, personal relationship with Jesus. God has given Cynthia an anointing to teach women how to enter the secret place with the Father. By correlating time in the secret place as a date with Jesus, Cynthia puts into perspective, key spiritual teachings. Her personal stories and biblical applications make this book relatable and powerful. I have personally seen Pastor Cynthia divine teachings first hand. The ladies at our church have held date nights with Jesus and found them to be life-changing. *Date Night with Jesus* will help lead you to a more intimate relationship with Jesus. It is a powerful book, that will change the way you approach time with God."

--Pastor Peggy Cowan
Author of "Living in the Promise"
J1:10 Ministries

"Pastor Cynthia Burton has written a God-inspired book about women developing intimacy with God.

We all know how busy life gets and how easy it is to overlook quality time with the ones we love the most.

Cynthia desires that *Date Night with Jesus* will compel and draw God's girls into a deep and intimate relationship with our Heavenly Dad. Cynthia provides direction on preparing for these very special encounters with God.

Each date provides focus points to ponder and reflect on; she encourages us to go deeper into His presence, to listen for His voice and to build a close relationship with Him.

Each date night ends with a special message of love from our date, God.

This book is not just an idea that Cynthia dreamed up. This book is a God-inspired idea developed over time as Cynthia and her church ladies enjoyed date nights with God and were mightily touched and impacted by their deepening relationships with God."

--Linda Renouf - New Zealand, Author, Gems for your Journey-A testimony to the faithfulness of God, our ever-present help in time of need.

"*Date Night with Jesus* will be just like a divine smile for your overcharged life. Cynthia

Burton shares her unique perspective on walking with Jesus in the midst of life's most chaotic situations. Jesus' love for you is greater than you know. It extends beyond what you can conceive or imagine. Just as you cannot measure the universe, you cannot fathom the limits of His love for you.

Personally, this devotional has ministered to me as a minister, and a mother caught up with the pressures of life. Through this devotional, you will discover a deeper, more intimate relationship with Jesus.

Jesus is waiting to reveal His love and power in every area of your life from your greatest tragedies to your smallest concerns. Her biblical insights will charge you with new energy and help you grow closer to Jesus. One of the most wonderful things about Jesus is that He lives in us and wants to be with us. Discover the joy of being with Jesus through this devotional."

--Karen Perez Associate Pastor and Co-founder of Jesus Christ the Glorious Savior Int'l. Ministry Philippines

"This book is a must read and will increase your relationship with God. As you read and apply this book to your life, you will be changed by the glory of God. What a life changing book that will powerfully make an influence in your life and impact your church and community."

--Rev. Karen Taylor
Cross Tabernacle Church, Terre Haute, IN
Co-founder Gilgal Ministries

"My colleague in ministry and good friend, Cynthia Burton, has not just written a good book for your reading pleasure, but her release of *Date Night with Jesus*, is an *experience*. With it, you will experience the beautiful *secret place* where you will fellowship with our Creator and the Lover of your soul. This book should be taken one chapter at a time. Read it. Absorb it. Pray it. Soaking in His presence and His love for you, as He 'sings over you!' Let me encourage you—don't just read it—experience it!"

--Tammy Oliver
Pastor's Wife, Worship Leader, Director of Music & Drama Ministries
First Assembly of God, Delphi, Indiana

"Pastor Cynthia once ministered at our lady's conference in Belfast, N. Ireland on this topic of a date night with Jesus. Many of the ladies myself included were encouraged because of this message to go on a pursuit of intimacy and greater relationship. The effects of those days remain in our lives, and we are forever changed. I am thankful for this book and this much-needed revelation. The contents are now available for a deposit for such a time as this and for those that cannot be imparted to on a personal level.

In essence, this book tells the story of someone who pursues the presence of God and then releases what she has received to enable us to enter the secret place and journey towards our own intimate set apart time with God which, in turn, makes us hungry for more and more. The disciples had the same understanding John 6:68 *'Lord, to whom shall we go? You have the words of eternal life.'"*
--Pastor Mardy Dunlop
Karmel City Church, Belfast, Ireland

"Having known Cynthia for almost 25 years, it has been a joy to see her grow in Christ. Cynthia knows the subject of intimacy with God because of the time she has spent with Him. It is her heart to encourage and help women to develop their relationship with Father God. In this book, Cynthia gives practical insights that will help you enter into His Presence."
--Rev. Cheryl Dean Church on the Rock, Batesville, IN

"The journey that Cynthia Burton takes us through in this daily devotional is primed to lead us to new levels in our relationship with Jesus! I love how *Date Night with Jesus* inspires with the Word, gives practical steps in experiencing the presence of the Holy Spirit, and prepares our hearts to hear from our Father in a safe place where intimacy is natural.

I am honored to call her friend and elated to see God using her gifts in ways that impact the Kingdom of God for such a time as THIS!"

--Kim Sharp Assemblies of God Ordained Minister, Director of Women's Ministries at Grace Assembly

"Not only has Cynthia written this amazing book titled *Date Night with Jesus*, but she has also lived it. Through its pages, you will be inspired and challenged to go deeper with our Lord Jesus Christ."

--Randall E. Burton Senior Pastor at Northview Church in Columbus, Indiana, Founder and President of Zebulun Ministries Inc. Author of the books River Rising & The Seed.

Date Night

with

Jesus

*"Your intimacy with God
is measured by the time
You spend with Him."*

Cynthia D. Burton

Date Night with Jesus
Cynthia D. Burton
Copyright © 2018 Cynthia D. Burton

Unless otherwise indicated, all Scripture quotations are from the New King James Version ®, © 1990, 1995 by Thomas Nelson Publishers, Nashville, Tennessee, Used by Permission. All rights reserved.

ISBN-13: 978-1985447813
ISBN-10: 1985447819

For Worldwide Distribution
Printed in the United States of America
First Edition Printing 2018

Contact Author at:
2584 Lafayette Ave., Columbus, IN 47201
812-343-6450
Email: secretarycin@sbcglobal.net

Word 2 Word Publishing
Word2wordministries@gmail.com
Sikeston, Missouri

Dedication

To my husband Randall.
You have encouraged, supported, and
inspired me to follow the leading of
God's voice and to obey Him no
matter the cost.
I love you!

Contents

Introduction

[1]The book, "Secrets of the Secret Place" by Bob Sorge has impacted my life in such a way, that I will never be the same. In the chapter, "The Secret of the Shut Door," Bob says, *"The secret place is your portal to the throne, the place where you taste of heaven itself."* Bob also says, *"To get there, all you have to do is shut your door."*

I thought I would put in to practice what I had read. So, I cleared my schedule and announced to everyone that I was going to go pray. As I opened the door to the secret place, I instantly knew this was going to be a significant time. When I shut the door, my whole being was jumping. Then I spoke out loud to the Lord, *"Well here I am."* I turned on some worship music and began to just sway at first. I was focusing on Jesus and how much I loved Him. Before I even knew what happened, I was dancing all over the room. I felt like I was in the throne room of heaven, and I could not stop dancing and worshipping my Lord. All of a sudden, I heard a loud voice in my spirit say, *"I want this with all my daughters."* I immediately stopped and laughed as I spoke out loud, *"And how am I responsible for that?"* The Lord very softly said, *"Do you trust me? If you do, I will show you."*

That day began a new journey for the ladies of my church and me. We began to have date nights with Jesus. These date nights were a time that we set aside, corporately, just to be with Him. There was usually a theme for the evening and one rule; once we went into the secret place room, we were not allowed to talk, pray, or prophecy over one another. The goal was to experience His presence, one on one with Him. The love and intimacy with our Father transformed both myself and the ladies from my church. I must admit that I had not experienced the depth of God's love and that level of intimacy with Him in the past; at least not the way I have now. Now, I must have time with God in the secret place. And, when I go to that place, it makes me hungry for more the next time. Many time's I can't get past just laying on my face in His presence for hours. I feel like I hear Him more clearly now. It is amazing how time with Him clears away the cobwebs of life.

I truly believe God wants to be with all His daughters, and that is why I am writing this book. I pray that you are compelled and drawn to the secret place, and while you are there, may you find out just how much He loves you and wants to be with you. Your journey begins today!

Crossing the Threshold

In today's world *busyness* is an enemy of the secret place. It can be such a challenge to find time for prayer and being with God. The significance of crossing the threshold of your secret place is huge. Once you cross it physically then comes the fight between the spirit and the mind. The definition of a threshold is the plank, stone, or piece of timber, which lies under a door, especially of a dwelling house, church, temple, or the like; the doorsill; hence, entrance; gate; door. This definition refers to a physical threshold. But, I believe that we also must cross another threshold to get into the Holy of Holies. And, that is stepping from our mind (which is our soul) into the spirit.

As you cross the threshold (both physically and spiritually) of your secret place, allow everything from the world to drop off. Romans 8:5-6 says, *"For those who live according to the flesh set their minds on the things of the flesh, but those who live according to the Spirit, the things of the Spirit. For to be carnally minded is death, but to be spiritually minded is life and peace."*

Do you trust God enough to allow the Spirit of God access to your mind? If you want life and peace in your mind, you must give up the desire to hold onto worldly thoughts such as anger, frustration, fear, and any other negative thoughts. It is a choice we make to keep our minds on worldly, fleshly things or to allow the Spirit of God to renew our mind daily. Romans 12:2 says, *"And do not be conformed to this world, but be transformed by the renewing of your mind, that you may prove what is that good and acceptable and perfect will of God."*

Our mind can be the door (or threshold) that allows us to enter the secret place or it can prevent us from entering in. Don't let your mind prevent you from crossing the threshold of the Holy of Holies-- your secret place.

You see, God doesn't want anything to come between you and Him. Exodus 23:21 says, *"Pay attention to him and listen to what he says. Do not rebel against him; he will not forgive your rebellion since my Name is in him."* (NIV) He is jealous for our attention. In Exodus 20, it is listed as one of the ten commandments. God is serious about wanting ALL our attention.

Getting Started

As you prepare for each of your date nights, consider incorporating your (5) senses. God created our five senses, and we use them to function every day. God can use these senses to minister to you in ways you may not realize.

[2]In a recent study My son, Eric did extensive research on the five senses. Here are some of his findings:

Revelation 3:20 NLT *"Look! I stand at the door and knock. If you hear my voice and open the door, I will come in, and we will share a meal together as friends."*

All five senses are used in this passage:

LOOK

HEAR

OPEN (with your hands)

SHARE A MEAL (Taste and smell).

Using all five senses, we have completeness in the relationship between God and us. He wants our whole sensory system to be enveloped with our relationship to Him.

Look- To see

Matthew 6:22 NLT, *"Your eye is a lamp that provides light for your body. When your eye is good, your whole body is filled with light."*

Hear

Deuteronomy 4:12 NLT, *"And the LORD spoke to you from the heart of the fire. You heard the sound of his words but didn't see his form; there was only a voice."*

Touch

Mark 6:56 NLT, *"Wherever he went--in villages, cities, or the countryside--they brought the sick out to the marketplaces. They begged him to let the sick touch at least the fringe of his robe, and all who touched him were healed."*

Smell

Genesis 2:7 NLT, *"Then the LORD God formed the man from the dust of the ground. He breathed the breath of life into the man's nostrils, and the man became a living person."*

Taste

Psalm 34:8 NLT, *"Taste and see that the LORD is good. Oh, the joys of those who take refuge in him!"*

Preparation for your date nights:

Hearing – Music (include music that will take you into deep worship.)

Smelling – Candles, flowers

Touching – Objects (that go along with the theme) to touch and examine.

Tasting – Edible items that you can taste that go with the theme.

Seeing – What you see helps you absorb what God is speaking to you.

This is a VERY special date!

Some women have never been on a date. For others, it has been years since they have dated. I would encourage you to make each of these dates a special time with your Lord. First of all, plan a time when there will be no one else around. You will want at least an hour or maybe two. Use some of the above items to enhance your time with your Lord. Keep in mind that these things are for your benefit. They will not make God show up any quicker, but they may help you connect.

A Night with Jesus

As you sit down in the presence of God, begin to focus your attention on Him and all that He has done for you. Begin to see how frail you are and how strong He is. Allow the things of this world to slip away as you come close to His throne; knowing that only this moment with your King matters. Begin to speak of your love and adoration for Him. Tell Him that nothing else is more important than being with Him. Let your Lord know that you want nothing from Him except just to be with Him. Read this passage in Psalm 91 and allow it to sink into your spirit.

Psalm 91
You who sit down in the High God's presence,
spend the night in Shaddai's shadow,
Say this: "GOD, you're my refuge.
I trust in you, and I'm safe!"
That's right—he rescues you from hidden traps,
shields you from deadly hazards.
His huge outstretched arms protect you—
under them you're perfectly safe;
his arms fend off all harm.
Fear nothing—not wild wolves in the night,

not flying arrows in the day,
Not disease that prowls through the darkness,
not disaster that erupts at high noon.
Even though others succumb all around,
drop like flies right and left,
no harm will even graze you.
You'll stand untouched, watch it all from a distance,
watch the wicked turn into corpses.
Yes, because GOD's your refuge,
the High God your very own home,
Evil can't get close to you,
harm can't get through the door.
He ordered his angels
to guard you wherever you go.
If you stumble, they'll catch you;
their job is to keep you from falling.
You'll walk unharmed among lions and snakes,
and kick young lions and serpents from the path.
14-16 'If you hold on to me for dear life,' says GOD,
'I'll get you out of any trouble.
I'll give you the best of care
if you'll only get to know and trust me.
Call me, and I'll answer, be at your side in bad times;
I'll rescue you, then throw you a party.
I'll give you a long life,
give you a long drink of salvation!'
The Message(MSG)

Trust

As you go deeper in His presence, allow yourself to trust Him totally. All He wants from you is to be completely dependent on Him. Just as a baby is dependent on its mother, so should you depend on the Lord; even when you do not understand why He allows things to happen to you.

Proverbs 3:5 says, *"Trust in the Lord with all your heart and lean not on your own understanding."* (NIV)

To trust the Lord, you must first be willing not to understand. Unfortunately, most of us want to understand what is happening. We think that will help us cope better. However, God wants us to give that lack of understanding to Him and trust Him with it. He wants us to give Him the very things that we hold tightest to. Those things we hold on to will never give us peace. Every time I have given something to the Lord that I didn't understand, He rewarded me with peace. Such a warm blanket of His glory came over me and engulfed my whole being. Isaiah 26:3 says, *"You will keep in perfect peace those whose minds are steadfast because they trust in you."* (NIV) He loves it when you trust Him.

Safety

Know that you are safe in His presence. Psalm 46:1 says, *"God is our refuge and strength, an ever-present help in trouble."* (NIV) God is our mighty protector. You have given him access to all your pain, and now He will cover you with His protection.

You have set God up to show off His majesty and power.

The trust that we talked about earlier is a path that leads to the safety of God. It's a path that is not easy to get to. It's a painful path that leads to victory. When you are in Him, there is no safer place. Hebrews 13:5 says He will never leave us or forsake us. That means that He will not leave us helpless. He will never leave us behind or abandon us.

Relationship

As you sit in the presence of God, begin to listen for His voice. Each time you come to the secret place to connect with God, you will become more familiar with His voice. Merriam Webster defines the relationship as *the state of being related or connected.* To have a relationship with God is to connect with Him. The more time you connect with him, the deeper your relationship with Him will be. Relationships grow over time. Just as a man and a woman need time for their relationship to grow, your relationship with God needs time to grow as well. There is no shortcut in this relationship. Each time you come to the secret place, you are growing your relationship. Your intimacy with God is measured by the time you spend with Him, and as your relationship with God grows, you will become familiar with His voice. You will become clearer about what the Father's will is for your life.

My Child,

I've been watching and waiting for the moment that you would come to be with Me in the secret place. You will not regret the time that you spend with Me. It will change your life. You have chosen to be in the most important place that you could be today--in My Presence.

When I created you, I smiled. The day you were born, My heart leaped. I knew that this world needed someone special like you. You are unique, and no one else is exactly like you. I have put gifts and talents in you, to be used for my glory. I watched you grow into a young woman, and I saw the good and the bad things in your life.

It is not my will that you experience suffering, rejection, or fear of any kind. The enemy tries to defeat you with these things. But, he will not win. I have seen you hurting and confused about my Love, and that makes Me sad. Because I am only capable of loving and I love you more than you could understand. My love for you will never cease. Even if you reject me, I will love you.

I am the God of FREEDOM and LIFE. If you allow me to break those holds in your life, I will. If you trust me, I will never let you down. It will be My greatest joy to see you free from the enemy's clutches.

Now come to Me and trust Me with it all. Trust that you are safe in My presence. If you want to know My will for your life, then come to this place often, and see what I will do.

Love,

Your Heavenly Father

Moments of Reflection

_____

_____

_____

_____

_____

_____

_____

_____

_____

_____

_____

_____

_____

_____

_____

_____

_____

Date 2

Purity

As you spend time with God in the secret place, you will begin to see how valuable you are to Him.

The word value has several meanings. Value means worth or desirability. Value is that quality of anything which is desirable or useful. It is to have a high opinion, to appreciate, respect or to cherish and treasure. You may not realize it, but you are a treasure to God. He desires to be with you. The scripture in Matthew 13:46 says, *"Who when he had found one pearl of great price, went and sold all that he had, and bought it."* (KJV) You are that pearl of great price. Pearls symbolize value and worth. Bridal gowns often have pearls on them. Pearls symbolize the bride's value and worth to her groom. The white symbolizes light, goodness, innocence, and purity. The color white is perfection.

Do you Remember your wedding day, or have you ever been in a wedding? Everything had to be perfect, your hair, nails, makeup, and dress. You made sure you were perfect. The goal was to WOW the Groom.

I remember my wedding day. As I walked down the aisle, I saw my groom with the biggest smile on his face. I knew he was pleased and at that moment all his attention was on me. Isaiah 61:10 says, *"I will greatly rejoice in the LORD, my soul shall be joyful in my God; for he hath clothed me with the garments of salvation, he hath covered me with the robe of righteousness, as a bridegroom decketh himself with ornaments, and as a bride adorneth herself with her jewels."* (KJV)

The word adorn is the Bride getting herself ready for the groom. She prepares herself for her wedding day. So, why do we think it unnecessary to prepare ourselves for the Lord?

Ephesians 1:4 says, *"According as he hath chosen us in him before the foundation of the world, that we should be holy and without blame before him in love:"* (KJV)

So, how do you prepare to be with Him? The first thing is to give your life to Him. If you died tonight would you go to heaven? If not, today can be a new beginning for you. God will wash away all your sin and make you pure and holy for His Glory.

Tell God you are sorry for ALL your sins, give your life to him and confess Jesus is the son of God. Then turn from your ways and live each day God's way. Romans 10:9-10 tells us, *"If you declare with your mouth, "Jesus is Lord," and believe in your heart that God raised him from the dead, you will be* saved. *[10] For it is with your heart that you believe and are justified, and it is with your mouth that you profess your faith and are saved."* (NIV)

When the bride walks down the aisle, her goal is to POSITION herself beside her groom. She positions herself to be with him. Nothing can stop her from getting in the position that will change her life; as we should also *position* ourselves to be with our God. When we prepare and position ourselves to be IN HIS presence, He rejoices.

Isaiah 62:5 says, *"as a bridegroom rejoices over his Bride, so will your God rejoice over thee."*(NIV)

Psalm 147:11 says, *"The Lord taketh pleasure in them that fear him, in those that hope in his Mercy."* (KJV)

Jeremiah 32:41 says, *"I will rejoice over them to do them good...with my whole heart and with my whole soul."* (KJV)

Zephaniah 3:17 says, *"He will take great delight in you...will rejoice over you with singing."*(NIV) He sings over us! Did you hear that? God sings over us! I don't know about you, but I want God to sing over me.

Song of Solomon 2:10 says, *"My beloved spoke, and said to me, 'Rise up, my love, my fair one, And come away.'"* What a loving call!

Maybe you think this is too much for you. Maybe You feel too sinful and unworthy to be so loved, too defiled to be called *My fair one.* The truth is, we are, but He loves us enough to clean us up and make us righteous and holy. Only He can do that.

Ephesians 5:27 says, *"That he might present her to himself a glorious church, not having spot, or wrinkle, or any such thing; but that she should be holy and without blemish."*

I truly believe God wants to be with all His daughters. I pray that you are compelled and drawn to the secret place, and while you are there, may you find out just how much He loves you and wants to be with you!

My Beloved,

You are My precious one, and I am so pleased that you are here with me. I cherish our times together. You are of utmost importance to Me. When you speak to Me, I bend my ear down to hear every word that you speak. Don't you understand how valuable you are to Me?

I remember the day that you submitted and gave your heart and life to Me. Oh, what a celebration we had in heaven! The angels rejoiced when you repented and gave your life to Me. No matter what your past or how many sins you committed, they were all washed away. In fact, I do not even remember them. But, unfortunately, you do. My sweet daughter, there are things from your past that you have not forgiven yourself for, even though I did. You continuously remember them. Will you allow me to take the guilt and shame from you? I will do it if you will trust Me. As you lay them down at My feet, My peace will cover you. Can you feel the healing in your heart beginning? I am making you pure and new My daughter.

I am overjoyed that you have decided to leave that baggage behind. Do you hear the song that I am singing? It's a song about you. I am singing and rejoicing over you now. Let My joy flood your soul. You are free. You are free from all that the enemy has deceived you into believing. It was all a lie. Nothing about it was true. My joy can be your joy too. You deserve it because YOU are a daughter of the King. It is your inheritance. Now, receive it and walk in it. Walk into the life that I have for you; a life full of righteousness, peace, and joy.
Love,
Your King (God)

Moments of Reflection

Date 3

See Me

"Who redeems your life from the pit and crowns you with love and compassion." Psalm 103:4

Remember Redemption

The drops of Jesus blood were real drops of blood. There are approximately 120,000 drops of blood in a human body. The drops of Jesus' blood were real drops of blood, and thousands of drops of His blood poured out for us. In reality, Jesus' body was bleeding to death, but in the Spirit, the blood of Jesus' was God's Love being poured out. God loved us so much, that He was willing to sacrifice His very own Son for our sins. Every drop of blood that poured out of Jesus' body was also God pouring out His love on us. Romans 5:6-8 says, *"You see, at just the right time, when we were still powerless, Christ died for the ungodly. [7] Very rarely will anyone die for a righteous person, though for a good person someone might possibly dare to die. [8] But God demonstrates his own love for us in this: While we were still sinners, Christ died for us.*" (NIV)

The drops of Jesus' blood formed a puddle at the foot of the cross. In the spirit, the drops formed a river of God's love. Allow that river of love to pour over you today. Think about how MUCH you are loved. Spend some time wrapped in the warmth of your Father's Love. As you worship Him, remember the cross. Remember the blood and remember redemption. *"For the message of the cross is foolishness to those who are perishing, but to us who are being saved, it is the power of God."* I Corinthians 1:18.

Allow God to comfort your heart as you give ALL your pain to Him. He loves you and wants you to have freedom from anything that stands in the way of your being with Him. *"For you have delivered my soul from death, my eyes from tears, and my feet from falling."* Psalm 116:8.

Pray that God would help you see what He wants you to see. *"Open my eyes, that I may see wondrous things from your law."* Psalm 119:18.

Pray that God would make you hungry to read His Word. Do you feel the weight of His word? I pray that you would also feel the weight of His Glory as you pray and seek Him. *"Or do you think that the scripture says in vain, the Spirit who dwells in us yearns jealously?"* James 4:5 *"For whatever things were written before were written for our learning, that we through the patience and comfort of the scriptures might have hope."* Romans 15:4.

Pray that God will help you to show the light of Jesus that is in you. *"You are the light of the world. A city that is set on a hill cannot be hidden."* Matthew 5:14 *"That you may become blameless and harmless, children of God without fault in the midst of a crooked and perverse generation, among whom you shine as lights in the world."* Philippians 2:15.

At some point during this date, if God speaks a word to you or you get freedom in an area in your life, write it down. Praise God for fresh revelation. *"For I neither received it from man, nor was, I taught it, but it came through the revelation of Jesus Christ."* Galatians 1:12 *"...so that you come short in no gift, eagerly waiting for the revelation of our Lord Jesus Christ."* I Corinthians 1:7.

Pray that God will give you His desires. When we allow Him to fill our heart with good, then we will give out good to others. You are a beautiful treasure to God. *"A good man out of the good treasure of his heart brings forth good, and an evil man out of the evil treasure of his heart brings forth evil. For out of the abundance of the heart his mouth speaks."* Luke 6:45.

Be FREE to worship and praise God however you choose. It's time to put your praise on! *"Lift up a banner on the high mountain, raise your voice to them; wave your hand, that they may enter the gates of the nobles.*" Isaiah 13:2. "*Rejoice in the Lord, O you righteous! For praise from the upright is beautiful.*" Psalm 33:1. "*My lips shall greatly rejoice when I sing to you, and my soul, which you have redeemed.*" Psalm 71:23.

My Daughter,

I am overjoyed that you are here. I have been waiting patiently for you to come and be with Me in the secret place. My eyes are always on you. Everywhere you go, I see you. When I see your eyes lifted up in prayer, My eyes lock onto yours. Do you see me? Do you know that my heart feels every tear that falls from your eyes? I see every smile on your face. And when you smile, I smile. You are My beautiful creation, and I love it when you worship Me.

It breaks My heart when you doubt what you are worth. I paid the ultimate price to prove to you how valuable you are My beloved. I have loved you with My life. Whenever you feel insecure about who you are, look to the cross. Nothing you could say or do in this life will change the way I feel for you. I gave My life to free you from the power of sin and allow you to live life to the fullest. Remember the cross My love, and you will never again doubt your worth.
Love,
Your Heavenly Father

Moments of Reflection

Date 4

Setting the Table of the Lord

On your date today, you will be sitting at the King's table. If you want a change in your life, you must spend time at His table.

Ronald Reagan said, "All great change begins at the dinner table." What a powerful statement.

The table is the center of the home. Psalm 128:3 says, *"Your wife will be like a fruitful vine within your house; your children will be like olive shoots around your table."*

When you are hungry in the natural, you go to the table to eat. When you are spiritually hungry, you go to the Lord's table to eat. John 6:35 says, *"Then Jesus declared, "I am the bread of life. Whoever comes to me will never go hungry, and whoever believes in me will never be thirsty."*

As you sit down to eat, you look to see if the dishes are full of food. Then you take a spoon and dip it into the food to eat. Before you put your hands on the food, you wash them. You wouldn't eat with dirty hands. It is the same way with our spiritual life. When we sit at the Lord's table, we examine our hearts to see if any unclean thing is there. If there is a need, we should quickly repent. Psalm 24:3-5, *"Who may ascend the mountain of the LORD? Who may stand in his holy place? [4]The one who has clean hands and a pure heart, who does not trust in an idol or swear by a false god. [5]They will receive blessing from the LORD and vindication from God their Savior."*

Set the Table with His presence

First, we must make a place and time to meet with God. The table is a symbol of a meeting place. God wants to meet with us. He wants us to make a place for Him in our lives; to prepare for His Glory to come. The word SET means to reside or permanently stay, abide, continue, dwell, have habitation, inhabit, lay, place, remain and rest. Even from the very beginning of time, God set up the Garden of Eden for Adam and Eve to meet with Him. Also, Moses met with God in the tabernacle or tent of meeting. The phrase has the meaning of a place for a fixed meeting. In Exodus 25:22, the Bible says, *"there I will meet with thee, and I will commune with thee from above the mercy seat;"* in Exodus 30:6 it says, *"before the mercy seat that is over the testimony, where I will meet with thee;"* Ex. 40:22-

23 says, *"Moses placed the table in the tent of meeting on the north side of the tabernacle outside the curtain and set out the bread on it before the Lord, as the Lord commanded him."* (NIV)

Do you have your table set to meet with Him? If so, what does that table setting look like? Maybe you have wrong things on your table; things like greed, selfishness, anger, bitterness, etc....

1 Corinthians 10:21 says, *"You cannot drink the cup of the Lord and the cup of demons too; you cannot have a part in both the Lord's table and the table of demons."* As you sit in the presence of God, examine your heart. Is it pure? Do you have a right spirit? If God reveals things to you that you need to remove, do not resist. Quickly repent.

Sit at the Table of His presence

When you sit down at a table that means you are hungry. Have you ever experienced true hunger? I have. Your stomach begins to growl and make noises. All you can think about is when you can eat and what you will eat. Hunger is a very powerful sensation. Hunger can drive people to do things they never thought they would do. Are you hungry for God? Do you desire to be in His presence? Matthew 5:6 says, *"Blessed are they which do hunger and thirst after righteousness: for they shall be filled."*

Mary understood the importance of sitting at the feet of her Lord. She did not allow her duties to keep her from being with the One she loved. Her hunger for God was greater than her hunger for food. She laid down her towel and laid at Jesus' feet. Luke 10:38-42 says, *"Now it happened as they went that He entered a certain village; and a certain woman named Martha welcomed Him into her house. And she had a sister called Mary, who also sat at Jesus' feet and heard His word. But Martha was distracted with much serving, and she approached Him and said, 'Lord, do You not care that my sister has left me to serve alone? Therefore, tell her to help me.' And Jesus answered and said to her, 'Martha, Martha, you are worried and troubled about many things. But one thing is needed, and Mary has chosen that good part, which will not be taken away from her."*

Martha allowed her duties to stand in the way of being with Jesus. Do you want to be like Martha or like Mary? Break off every distraction and duty from your mind as you enter the throne room. Realize that He is all that truly matters at this moment.

So much can happen to you when you sit in the presence of the King. Jesus Delivered a man from demons while in His presence. Luke 8:35 tells us, *"The people went out to see what had happened; and they came to Jesus and found the man from whom the demons had gone out, sitting down at the feet of*

Jesus, clothed and in his right mind; and they became frightened." In His presence salvation, deliverance and blessings come. More than we could ever think or imagine comes when we are in His presence.

Stay at the Table in His presence

You may ask, "How do I stay in His presence?" First, let's look at the word *stay*. Here are some synonyms that may help: remain, continue, dwell, cling, abide, persist, LIVE. Stay is a Verb. It is an action. So, to stay means I must consciously go to that place. It means to live in His presence. Psalm 91:1 says, *"Whoever dwells in the shelter of the Most High will rest in the shadow of the Almighty."* (KJV) When He lives in me, everything I do should be from my relationship with Him. So, I can tap into what He instills in me during our secret place or date nights.

As you come into His presence, examine your heart. Is there anything that you need to remove? Allow ALL the Lord has for you to seep into your whole being. Take it all in because at any moment you may need to tap into what you have received. You can DWELL in that place with Him.

My Lovely One,
You look so frail and thin. How long has it been since you sat at my table and dined with Me? I see you wandering from here to there looking for

sustenance. But, you will never be full when you eat of what the world has to offer. It will always leave you feeling hungry.

Are you hungry and thirsty for more of Me? I have set a table for you, and it is spread with all My goodness. It's a beautiful sight. It has everything you need. There is love on the table. Joy is overflowing on the table for you. Oh, and My peace is there too. Longsuffering is there along with bowls of kindness, goodness, faithfulness, gentleness, and self-control. I am able to do more than you could ever think or imagine.

You, are welcome to take as much as you need and come back as often as you'd like. My table is always set and waiting for you. You are my daughter, and you are always welcome at my table. Did you know that you can even live at my table? That's right! You can take it with you wherever you go because I am in you and you are in Me. Now come and sit with Me and let's share a cup of fellowship as we dine.
With Love,
God

Moments of Reflection

_____
_____
_____
_____
_____
_____
_____
_____
_____
_____
_____
_____
_____
_____
_____
_____
_____
_____
_____
_____
_____
_____
_____
_____
_____
_____

Date 5

The Voice of the Lord

"The voice of the Lord is over many waters."
Psalm 29:3

When you come into His presence, enter with the intent to hear what He wants to speak to you. Lay down every distraction that comes to mind. Focus on Jesus and Him alone. As you worship, He will begin to speak to you. Write down everything you hear from Him. Then compare what He speaks to you with the Word of God. If you are hearing from Him, it will line up with the Word of God. What He says to you will never disagree with what the Bible says.

I have heard many people ask this question, "How do I know if I am hearing God's voice?"

John 10:27 says, *"My sheep hear My voice, and I know them, and they follow Me."* (KJV) Before you can hear, you must be still and listen. If you are constantly talking, you will not hear His voice. If you are constantly telling Him your desires and your requests, then you will not be able to hear His answers. When we only hear our own desires over, and over in our mind, we are blocking out His voice. Eventually, all we hear is our own desires. Our desires can become like white noise, blocking out what we need to hear. We need to be willing to lay down our own agendas, dreams, and visions to hear Him. Is your voice drowning out His voice?

Luke 5:16 says, *"And he withdrew himself into the wilderness, and prayed."* (KJV) Even Jesus withdrew to lonely places to talk to His Father. He withdrew himself from every voice except His Father's voice.

To hear His voice, we must be in a relationship with Him. Just like our relationships, if we neglect or abandon them, the relationship will suffer. Why is it that we think we do not need to spend time building our relationship with God? Time must be an investment in every relationship. God is no different.

In Psalm 29:3-9 says, *"The voice of the LORD is over the waters; the God of glory thunders, the LORD thunders over the mighty waters. ⁴The voice of the LORD is powerful; the voice of the LORD is majestic. ⁵The voice of the LORD breaks the cedars; the LORD breaks in pieces the cedars of Lebanon. ⁶He makes Lebanon leap like a calf, Sirion like a young wild ox. ⁷The voice of the LORD strikes with flashes of lightning. ⁸The voice of the LORD shakes the desert; the LORD shakes the Desert of Kadesh. ⁹The voice of the LORD twists the oaks and strips the*

forests bare. And in his temple all cry, "Glory!"
(NIV)

The Psalmist David mentions *the Voice of the Lord* seven times. The number seven means completeness. David does this to portray God's power and glory. Thunder is a manifestation or symbol of God's voice. Job 37:2 says, *"Hear attentively the thunder of His voice, and the rumbling that comes from His mouth."* Other manifestations of God's voice are wind, earthquake, fire and even a still small voice. God's voice has been described as Mighty and a Voice of Multitudes.

But, how do we know if what we are hearing is God's voice? There are two Greek translations for *"word."*

The first word is:
Logos – Written word of God.

The second word is:
Rhema – Living or lifegiving word of God.

The Rhema Word and Logos Word will always agree with one another. Jesus is both the Written and Living Word of God. They will always be in harmony with one another. We measure what we are hearing with what the Word of God says. If what we hear differs from what God's Word says, we throw it out. If it is in alignment with the Word of God, and it is a life-giving Word, then we keep it.

God's voice has the power to change. His Voice parted the Red Sea. When He spoke to Moses to stretch out His hand, not only did the sea part but the Israelites went from looking at the face of death to walking into life. Exodus 14:26-27 says, *"Then the LORD said to Moses, "Stretch out your hand over the sea, that the waters may come back upon the Egyptians, on their chariots, and on their horsemen." And Moses stretched out his hand over the sea; and when the morning appeared, the sea returned to its full depth, while the Egyptians were fleeing into it. So, the LORD overthrew the Egyptians in the midst of the sea."* (AKJV)

Every time I have experienced God speaking to me, it has changed me. It is usually simple, but extremely powerful.

A few years ago, I was going through a difficult time. I felt alone and afraid. My life was changing, and I didn't know how to handle it. I began praying and telling the Lord all about it. When I finally gave up, I said, *"Lord I trust you."* After that, I became still and quiet. All I heard God saying was, *"I've got this."* Such warmth came over my whole being. I knew it was God comforting me and allowing me to feel His love and presence. I came away from that prayer time a changed woman. And, so can you.

Hearing God's voice changes us if we obey what He tells us. It is our responsibility after He has spoken to us, to do what He says to do. Have you ever had someone ignore something you told them to do? It's very frustrating, and it makes you not so eager to tell them the next time, right?

God expects us to listen and obey. We need to be careful not to ignore what God tells us. If we obey, we will gain the trust of the Lord, and He will speak to us more often.

My Daughter,

Oh, how I have longed to be with you. I have been here waiting for you. I think of you all the time. My thoughts of you outnumber the grains of sand. I know every hair on your head, and I painted every freckle on your face. Oh, how I love you so. If only you could see yourself as I see you.

Sometimes I know you are lonely and feel rejected by everyone, but did you know that I was here all the time. I am here now. Do you feel My breath on your cheek or My whisper in your ear? Do you sense My GLORY spilling out over you now? Be still and listen. Still, all your fears and doubts My child, for I am right here. I have not left you. Do not listen to the enemy's talk. Be still and listen to My Voice. I am here with you.

Trust Me and what I say in My Word to be true. You will find your answers when you find Me in the secret place. When you spend time with Me, My sweet princess, I will transform you into the woman I intended you to be all along. You can't do it on your own anymore. Don't you see, you need Me, and I need you.

Your Loving Father (God)

Moments of Reflection

_____
_____
_____
_____
_____
_____
_____
_____
_____
_____
_____
_____
_____
_____
_____
_____
_____
_____
_____

Date 6

Changed by the Glory

"And we all, who with unveiled faces contemplate the Lord's glory, are being transformed into his image with ever-increasing glory, which comes from the Lord, who is the Spirit."
2 Corinthians 3:18 (NIV)

Unveiled Face

Come into the secret place with an unveiled face. An unveiled face is one that is not blinded. It is open and uncovered. God wants the *real* you. He does not want you to come to Him hiding things. He made you and already knows everything about you. Isaiah 43:7 says, *"Even every one that is called by my name: for I have created him for my glory, I have formed him; yea, I have made him."* (KJV) The reason He wants you to come to Him with all your weaknesses revealed is to transform you into the person He wants you to become. When you come into His presence unwilling to face the weak areas of your life, He cannot take you any further.

The Lord's Glory

The Glory of God's presence will change you. If you have things in your life that you have never been able to overcome, then saturate yourself in His presence, and He will change you. You can't make the Glory come, but the Glory comes when you make time to be with Him. Every time I have experienced God's Glory, I have been changed.

Several years ago, lightning struck a tree in our front yard. My husband was standing at our picture window in our living room when it occurred. As he described it, the bright light flashed, and the crackling sound of the smoky trail of lightening aftermath whipped down the tree in just seconds. Since then, that tree has grown several feet higher. Today, you can still see the impact of the initial lightning strike, where it peeled the bark back all the way down to the trunk. It left a big hole at the point of impact, but the tree stands tall today.

Recently, we noticed that the point of impact on that tree had moved up higher over the years. It looks like that tree has one great big long scar going up toward the top. Here is the point-no matter how high you go up in life or ministry, the scars always go up with you, and those scars are reminders of our lightning bolt experiences. When you have that lightning bolt experience with God, it changes you forever.

Saul of Tarsus was CHANGED when lightning struck him. In Acts chapter 9 it says that he saw a bright light, was thrown from his donkey and heard the voice of God saying Saul, Saul why are you persecuting me? Paul repented and turned from his evil ways and followed God. He became the great apostle Paul who wrote two-thirds of the New Testament. Paul was changed by the powerful glory of God.

Also, the Glory CHANGED Mary of Magdalena. John 20 tells the story of Mary Magdalene at the tomb after Jesus was resurrected. Mary was the first person to see Jesus after the resurrection. At first, she did not recognize him. However, one word from the Voice changed everything. She easily recognized Him as he uttered her name, *"Mary."* That familiar voice gripped her heart, and instantly she cried "Rabboni!" She cast herself before her risen Lord with love and adoration.

What is *your* expression of love for Him? Mary's was *"Rabboni,"* which means master or teacher and was used as a Jewish title of respect. Have you found your expression of love for Him yet? Even in Jesus' glorified state, He remembered that she is special. Why? Her relationship with Him. After Jesus delivered her from seven demons, she left her life and followed him. She was devoted to Him. She spent much time with Him. Because of her relationship with Him, He made Himself known to her. In just a moment after He spoke her name, she went from grief to glory. She went from not knowing where they laid the body of her deceased Lord to KNOWING He was alive! Her state of mind was changed. Sadness, fear, and confusion were broken. In her grief, she met the Glory. Mary went from Glory to Glory. The Glory that she knew wasn't the only Glory. There was more to come when the Savior was resurrected in His glorified body. She was so used to the glory she had always known; she didn't recognize the More glory that was right with her!

Before His glorified state, she knew him as master/teacher. After His glorified state, she knew Him as her Master and Lord. Of all people, he chose her to be the first witness of the resurrection. She was the first person to witness the most important event in world history.

She didn't recognize Him. But He recognized her.

Transformed

It's simple really…when we spend time with Him, His Glory comes, and we are CHANGED or transformed. Sometimes we hear people say, "When the Glory comes, I will fall on my face." Or, "I cannot stand in His Glory." This is true, but He wants us to fall on our face first so that the Glory will come. When God is present, His Glory comes.

God can do the same for you. Do you need confusion broken off your life? He is waiting for you to be with Him. He wants to build a relationship with you, but if you don't meet with Him, how can you know His voice when He speaks your NAME!

My Child,

You may not know Me, but I know everything about you. I know when you sit down and when you rise up. I am familiar with all your ways. Even the very hairs on your head are numbered. For you were made in My image. In Me, you live and move and have your being. For you are My offspring. I knew you even before you were conceived. I chose you when I planned creation. You were not a mistake, for all your days are written in My Book. I determined the exact time of your birth and where you would live. You are fearfully and wonderfully made. I knit you together in your mother's womb and brought you forth on the day you were born.

I have been misrepresented by those who don't know Me. I am not distant and angry, but I am the complete expression of love. I desire to lavish My love on you. Simply because you are My child and I am your Father. I offer you more than your earthly father ever could. For I am the perfect father. Every good gift that you receive comes from My hand. For I am your provider and I meet all your needs.

My plan for your future has always been filled with hope because I love you with an everlasting love. My thoughts toward you are countless as the sand on the seashore. I rejoice over you with singing. I will never stop doing good to you. For you are My treasured possession. I desire to establish you with all My heart, and I want to show you great and marvelous things. If you seek Me with all your heart, you will find Me. Delight in Me and I will give you the desires of your heart. For it is I who gave you those desires. I can do more for you than you could imagine. For I am your greatest encourager.

I am also the Father who comforts you in all your troubles. When you are brokenhearted, I am close to you. As a shepherd carries a lamb, I have carried you close to my heart. One day I will wipe away every tear from your eyes, and I will take away all the pain you have suffered on this earth. I am your Father, and I love you even as I love My son, Jesus. For in Jesus, My love for you is revealed. He is the exact representation of My being. He came to demonstrate that I am for you, not against you and to tell you that I am not counting your sins. Jesus died so that you and I could be reconciled. His death was the ultimate expression of My love for you. I gave up everything I loved that I might gain your love. If you receive the gift of My son Jesus, you receive Me, and

nothing will ever separate you from My love again. Come home, and I'll throw the biggest party heaven has ever seen. I have always been Father and will always be Father. My question is... Will you be My child? I am waiting for you.
Love,
Your Dad Almighty God

Take some time to read and study these scriptures, and they will confirm the depth of the Lord's love for you. If you read and apply them, you *will* be changed.

Psalm 139:1, Psalm 139:2, Jeremiah 31:3,
Psalm 139:3, Matthew 10:29-31, Genesis 1:27,
Acts 17:28, Acts 17:28, Jeremiah 1:4-5,
Ephesians 1:11-12, Psalm 139:15-16, Acts 17:26,
Psalm 139:14, Psalm 139:13, Psalm 71:6,
John 8:41-44, 1 John 4:16, 1 John 3:1, Matthew 7:11,
Matthew 5:48, James 1:17, Matthew 6:31-33,
Jeremiah 29:11, Psalms 139:17-18, Zephaniah 3:17,
Jeremiah 32:40, Exodus 19:5, Jeremiah 32:41,
Jeremiah 33:3, Deuteronomy 4:29, Psalm 37:4,
Philippians 2:13, Ephesians 3:20,
2 Thessalonians 2:16-17, 2 Corinthians 1:3-4, Psalm 34:18, Isaiah 40:11, Revelation 21:3-4, Revelation 21:3-4, John 17:23, John 17:26,
Hebrews 1:3, Romans 8:31, 2 Corinthians 5:18-19,

2 Corinthians 5:18-19, 1 John 4:10, Romans 8:31-32,
1 John 2:23, Romans 8:38-39, Luke 15:7,
Ephesians 3:14-15, John 1:12-13, Luke 15:11-32

Moments of Reflection

_____
_____
_____
_____
_____
_____
_____
_____
_____
_____
_____
_____
_____
_____
_____
_____
_____
_____
_____
_____
_____
_____

Date 7

Survival Mode

I have a challenge for you today. As you enter the secret place, lay down your agenda. Put aside your own needs, desires, and expectations. Begin to see your life with kingdom eyes. Look at your life through the lens of God. This takes great discipline, especially if you have a lot going on in your life. But, I challenge you to focus on the kingdom of heaven. Focus on the cross. When you do this, God will give you a new perspective.

Many times, I have found myself simply going through the motions; trying to survive. It seemed I had tunnel vision and could not see past my circumstances. I knew things were happening in the lives of others, but I just couldn't get past my own stuff.

Maybe you are experiencing that right now. I call this Survival mode. Survival mode is when we have no vision for the future because we are just trying to get through today. Survival mode is not having the time to greet your neighbors because you do not even see them. They are hidden behind a veil in your mind. Your mind can only focus on the issues at hand. You have effectively cut off everything and everyone that would veer you away from surviving. When you are in survival mode, it becomes about self-preservation for you. It is ALL about you!

When you are in survival mode, your kingdom mission can be delayed or even stopped. Jesus did not have a survival mode mentality. He had a mission mentality. Even though He knew His physical life was coming to an end, He didn't look to the end. He lived every day with a mission to save, heal and deliver.

Luke 8:41-44, "And behold, there came a man named Jairus, and he was a ruler of the synagogue. And he fell down at Jesus' feet and begged Him to come to his house, [42] for he had an only daughter about twelve years of age, and she was dying. But as He went, the multitudes thronged Him. [43] Now a woman, having a flow of blood for twelve years, who had spent all her livelihood on physicians and could not be healed by any, [44] came from behind and touched the border of His garment. And immediately her flow of blood stopped."

Jesus healed people even as He was on the way to heal people. Though He faced death, He brought life.

Putting the mission of God first takes real discipline. Your mind, will, and emotions must submit to Kingdom thoughts. But, to do this, you will need to let go of those things that are about YOU; your hurts, fears, your past and even things like your own agendas, goals, and desires. *You may ask how in the world can I do that?*

What I do when I go to God is; I begin to focus on the throne room of God. As I move closer to Him, I know I must let things go. So, I drop them one by one. Finally, when I feel like I am at the throne of God, I examine what is left. What I have left is usually what is most important to me. God begins to show each thing in my hands, and then I lay it down at the feet of Jesus. I begin to tell the Lord how much I trust Him with these things that matter to me the most. Then, I turn around and walk away, knowing that God has them, and I can trust Him with it all. After I do this, my mind is free to focus on God's mission. I have nothing to hold me back from hearing my mission from heaven.

This is what *I* do to discipline my mind. For you, it may be different. There is no right or wrong way, but it is important that we learn to discipline our mind, will, and emotions so that we can be about the Father's business.

Jesus said we are the light of the world. Matthew 5:14-16 says, *¹⁴ You are the light of the world. A city that is set on a hill cannot be hidden. ¹⁵ Nor do they light a lamp and put it under a basket, but on a lampstand, and it gives light to all who are in the house. ¹⁶ Let your light so shine before men, that they may see your good works and glorify your Father in heaven.* We are to be the light of the world, but if we allow our stuff to get in the way, then we can snuff out our light.

Don't allow your *survivor mode* to get in the way of your going about the Father's business. Let your light shine brightly in a dark world!

To My Light,

This world is full of darkness. And many people do not know Me. I desire that every living person would come to know Me as their Lord and Savior. For this to happen, you must allow your light to shine. Your light is just as important as anyone else's light. Do not think that your light doesn't matter, it does! Everyone you come in contact with can see your light, and they are affected by it because your light is ME shining through you.

My daughter, when you allow the things of this world to cloud your mind, it dims your light and blocks out My voice. I need You more than you could ever realize. I need every part of you, especially your mind. I need your mind to be sober and clear, so that, your light can shine brightly on everyone you meet.

Look through My eyes and see what I see. I see lost and hurting people. Do you see them? I see people willing to do just about anything to survive. I have a mission for you, but you must first learn to see past yourself. When trials and issues arise, give them to Me. Do not take it upon yourself to solve everything. You are not able. It is only when you give those things to Me that answers come. I need you to have a clear mind, so you hear My voice.

You are the lamp, now let me light your path!
Love,
God

Moments of Reflection

_____

_____

_____

_____

_____

_____

_____

_____

_____

_____

_____

_____

_____

_____

_____

_____

_____

_____

_____

Reflection of Beauty

When you look in the mirror, what do you see? Do you only see flaws and glaring imperfections? Are you hiding behind a veil? Are you afraid of what you will see if you take an honest look at yourself? Do you immediately begin to pick out what you would like to change, or do you embrace what you see and find Jesus glowing and beaming back at you from the inside?

So many women cannot comfortably look in the mirror. They find it difficult to look themselves in the eye. When you look in your own eyes, there is nowhere to hide, and you cannot lie. So, to avoid seeing what you don't want to see, you don't look.

Most of us have heard the phrase, "Beauty is in the eye of the beholder." This means that it is the onlooker who determines what is beautiful. What I see as beautiful, you may not. We all have different opinions and ideas about what beauty is. Our experiences and even our culture help to shape our ideas. Not so with God. He does not see our appearance as beautiful or ugly.

God saw David differently than Samuel the Prophet saw him. God saw David differently than his own family saw him.

1 Samuel 16:7 says, *"But the LORD said to Samuel, "Do not consider his appearance or his height, for I have rejected him. The LORD does not look at the things people look at. People look at the outward appearance, but the LORD looks at the heart."* (NIV) God sees our heart and determines our beauty.

We live in a world that determines beauty by outward appearance. I have seen women that appear beautiful on the outside but are quite dark on the inside. It makes them ugly and unattractive. Just as I have also met women that do not appear to be attractive on the outside, but after getting to know them, their inward beauty shown through. The love and caring that emanates from their eyes makes them beautiful.

It is often easier to believe that about others, while harshly judging ourselves.

Years ago, the Lord spoke to me to look in the mirror. He instructed me to look into my own eyes. I had allowed the enemy to lie to me for years, and God finally confronted me with it. When I looked in the mirror, into my own eyes, it broke me. I began to cry because I didn't like what I saw. I saw the fear of man. I saw rejection. I saw unworthiness. But, as I saw those things, the Lord asked me this question,

"Are you my daughter?" I immediately knew what He meant. I said, "Yes, I am." He then told me to look in the mirror and declare that I was his daughter and that I was beautiful because *HE* IS BEAUTIFUL! And, if He lives in me then that makes me beautiful too.

Realizing this truth, I squared my shoulders, looked into my eyes in the mirror and pointed my finger at my own face. *"You stop this right now!"* I said. *"You are beautiful because your God lives inside you. You are the daughter of a King!"*

From that day, I vowed to remember that moment. I am a reflection of the beautiful God that I serve, and I purposed to honor Him by speaking well of His creation—Me! You, too, are a reflection of Jesus!

2 Corinthians 3:18 *And we all, who with unveiled faces contemplate the Lord's glory, are being transformed into his image with ever-increasing glory, which comes from the Lord, who is the Spirit.* (NIV)

When you finally grasp what this means, it will be very liberating for you. You will begin to see yourself differently. When someone compliments you, you will smile and say thank you. Your actions and reactions will show that you believe you are God's beautiful creation. It isn't a matter of pride. There is a difference between being prideful and thinking you are too good for someone or a situation and having a humble heart that is thankful God lives in you. You can be confident in knowing that YOU ARE A DAUGHTER OF THE KING and that you reflect His beauty.

My Beauty,

I am so pleased that you have set aside this time for us to be together. I have been longing to be with you. Do you know what it is like to watch and wait for someone you dearly love? Every day I expectantly wait for you. But many days my heart is so saddened that you do not show up. I look for you as a Bridegroom looks for his Bride.

I created you to worship, love and adore ME. My greatest desire is to have your worship and adoration. My heart is full when you draw near to Me. I want to give you all My favor and blessings if only you would sacrifice your selfish desires.

There is only one you, and I want ALL of you. You are a treasured possession of Mine. I am jealous of anything that takes you from Me. I love you more than you can understand. I love every single thing about you. Do you know that I smile when I think of you? Even if you do not love everything about yourself, I DO. You are My creation, My work, My joy.

When you say bad things about yourself, it hurts Me deeply. I am grieved when I see you filled with heaviness instead of joy. There are so many things that weigh heavy on you: like depression, loneliness, pride, selfish motives, lust, anger, lack of self-control, grief, rejection, worry and many more. It is not My will for you to live like this. In Psalm 55:22, I tell you to turn your burdens over to Me, and I will take care of you.

I spilled out my blood just for you. Do you see how much I love you? The pain and agony I experienced on the Cross was almost unbearable. I can hear the pounding of the nails and the cursing of the crowd, can you? The worst pain you can imagine does not touch the pain I experienced that day. But, I did it for you.

All that I ask in return is for your love, devotion, and praise. I paid the price for your salvation and your freedom from eternal death. That is why you are so precious to me.

Allow the warmth of my presence to cover you right now. I am bringing healing and life to the dead places that have been dead for a long time. Can you feel it? Allow MY Love to penetrate your heart and crowd out any hate, anger or fear. I am washing away your hurts as you soak in the River of my presence.

Do not be afraid my daughter, because I am with you. Trust me and know that I am your answer because I AM the GREAT I AM!
Your Loving Father

Moments of Reflection

Date 9

A Place of Rest

If you are feeling tired, weary, unfocused, and overwhelmed it's time to lay all that down at the feet of Jesus. *Matthew 11:28* says, *"Come to me, all you who are weary and burdened, and I will give you rest."* (NIV) It's time for you to rest. During your time with God, allow Him to fill you with His strength. Lay before Him, and soak in His presence.

Unfortunately, people do not know how to rest. Rest is almost a lost concept; especially here in the United States. In European countries, they know that rest is important.

When I was in Verona, Italy in 2013, I was amazed at how they viewed rest. They take rest seriously. So much so, that they close ALL their businesses down in the afternoon. There is *nothing* open during the afternoon hours.

The busy world we live in will consume us if we allow it. Therefore, we need a place to run and time to regroup. We need a place of safety; a Shiloh, a rest.

In Hebrew, the word Shiloh means, "a place of rest." It was a city in Ephraim and a temporary home of the Ark of the Covenant and the Tabernacle, the place where Samuel grew up.

Joshua 18:1 says, *"And the whole congregation of the children of Israel assembled together at Shiloh and set up the tabernacle of the congregation there. And the land was subdued before them."* (KJV)

Shiloh is also the prophetic name for Jesus. We all need a Shiloh. Some people call it a spiritual retreat or a sabbath rest. Whatever you want to call it, it is imperative to your wellbeing, to make sure you have this Shiloh.

Though we often do not realize it, sometimes, the most spiritual thing we can do is rest. My husband and I have sought out this type of rest many times. There are times that I only have an hour, so I retreat to my bathtub and soak my spirit and my body. There are times when I have a free evening or an entire day. So, I lock my doors, pull down the blinds and rest, pray and study.

However, there are times we need more than that. So, I schedule a two or three-day retreat in a cabin with no phones or TV. Then there are also times that I schedule a whole week away from home. Every time we have done this, we have been refreshed and rejuvenated. When we rest, revelation always comes. It amazes me how fresh revelation comes when we are rested. So, if you need fresh revelation, then take some time to rest. Get before the Lord, and I assure you revelation will come.

Even Jesus understood the need for rest. Mark 1:35 says, *"Very early in the morning, while it was still dark, Jesus got up, left the house and went off to a solitary place, where he prayed.* (NIV) and Mark 6:31-32 tells us, *"Then, because so many people were coming and going that they did not even have a chance to eat, he said to them, 'Come with me by yourselves to a quiet place and get some rest.' So, they went away by themselves in a boat to a solitary place."* (NIV)

If Jesus, being the son of God knew how important it was to take a Sabbath rest, then why would we do any different. When we take a Sabbath rest, we are telling the Father that we cannot make it on our own. We are surrendering and admitting that we need Him to rejuvenate us and make us strong. It is when we refuse to take a Sabbath rest that we are sending Him the message that we do not need Him. We are telling God, *"I can do it my way, on my own."*

I don't know about you, but I want God to know that I need Him. I want Him to make me strong!

My Child,

I see you flitting about here and there trying to keep up with your busy life. You look so tired and overwhelmed by the world. I have tried to get your attention, but you were so distracted that you did not notice. I have even spoken your name, but you have not heard.

55

So, come away with Me now to a place of peace and safety. Come into My presence. Take off every burden and every busy thought. Name them out loud as you release them to Me and allow Me to become your focus. All I want is you; all your weakness, all your fear, all your worry. I want it all. As you give it all to Me, you will begin to feel lighter. Do you feel the world's burdens being lifted off your shoulders? Now, I am covering you with My weight, the weight of My Glory. Do you feel My Glory? Just stay in my Glory and soak in My presence for a while. Remember, stay focused on Me.

There are things I want to speak to you; visions and dreams I want to give you. This is the place where you will find answers. This is the place you will receive strategies from me. This is the place that you will receive healing and encouragement. All that you ever needed or will ever need is found in this place; My Secret Place. When you are lonely, I will fill that void. When you are angry, I will give you joy. When you are sick, I will bring healing to your body. When your heart is hurting with grief and pain, I will bring you peace and comfort. When you have been rejected, I will accept you with open arms. When you have been victimized, I will love you with My most tender love.

I am and will ALWAYS be exactly what you need. From the moment you took your first breath,

until the moment you breathe your last, I will be there. I love you, My child.
Your Heavenly Father

Moments of Reflection

_____

_____

_____

_____

_____

_____

_____

_____

_____

_____

_____

_____

_____

_____

_____

_____

_____

_____

_____

_____

_____

_____

Date 10

Blessings and Stuff

As you enter the secret place today, focus on God's blessings. According to the Bible, blessing is; to speak well of, praise, extol, give thanks. To be spiritually blessed is to have an inner joy and peace that comes with being right with God. Happiness may be part of it, but the term happy has been overused and devalued. When we think of the word blessing, it can mean, God as a blessing, you were blessed or you blessed someone else.

Genesis 1:22 is the first mention of a blessing. When God blessed the sea creatures and birds, telling them to be fruitful and multiply in the earth.

Matthew 5 and Luke 6 describe the happy state of those who find their purpose and fulfillment in God. If you want your life to be blessed, then being right with God is the path to blessings.

Maybe you are going through something right now, and you wonder if your blessings will ever come. In Genesis 37-41 Joseph went from a prison to a platform. He went from prisoner to Governor.

Joseph had to go through some stuff to receive his blessing.

Being blessed is not necessarily the absence of responsibility nor is it the presence of freedom. Joseph was in prison. He did not have his freedom, but he was eventually elevated or blessed.

If you will stay the course, continue following God and keep your heart right, you will eventually see the blessings of the Lord. My husband Randall has said, *"When it comes to taking responsibility, the body of Christ wants a response from God without giving Him their ability. It's called response-ability for a reason. We want the Presence without a price. We want the glory without giving a gift. We want a cloud without having clout."*

Deuteronomy 28 says, to be blessed you must be obedient to the Lord's command daily. Faith comes by hearing and hearing by the word of God. What do you do after you receive a word from God? You, walk out your faith in obedience to that word.

Sometimes, we need to let go of what we have in order to get what God has for us.

Genesis 45:20, *"Also regard not your stuff; for the good of all the land of Egypt is yours."* (KJV)

What God had for the Israelites was more important than their stuff in Egypt. To receive their blessing, they had to be willing to leave their stuff behind.

We think getting a blessing (physical, spiritual, or financial) is in addition to what we already have, but God's blessing can mean starting over with only what He has for us. Our stuff can get in the way of God's stuff. This can mean our dreams and visions as well. We need to be willing to give God ALL our stuff. And sometimes the hardest thing to give him is our dreams and visions for our future.

I have seen this work in my own life. On one occasion, the Lord began speaking to my husband and I that we were too attached to our stuff. So, we agreed that we would start giving it away. That year we gave away our dining room table, some living room furniture, musical equipment, birthday money and 18% of our salary. Because of our heart, the Lord honored our giving, and we were blessed immensely. The Lord loves it when we have a heart to give.

2 Corinthians 9:7 *So let each one give as he purposes in his heart, not grudgingly or of necessity; for God loves a cheerful giver.*

Two of the most cheerful givers I know are my mom and dad. They have such a heart to give. I do not believe I know anyone else like them when it comes to giving tithes and offerings to the Lord. Every time they receive a financial blessing, the first thing my mom says is, *"Praise God! We get to tithe on this!"* They really love giving to the Lord. If you bless the Lord with your life, He will bless you, so that you can bless others.

Daughter,

When I think of you, I am blessed. I am a God who loves to lavish good things on His children. You may not understand where your life is going yet. You might think you are not blessed, but if you are in Me, then you are blessed. If you stay under the shadow of My wings, then you will be blessed. Stay under My covering when your life seems to be whirling out of control. Don't leave. Don't try to figure it out on your own. Stay with Me and walk with Me.

Give me your heart, your dreams, your hurt. Give me all of you. I am a jealous God, and I want all of you. If you trust Me, I will pour out My blessings on you. In Me, there is life. In Me, there is hope. When it seems that all is lost; have hope. I love to bring life to dead places. Remember, I am a God of healing, salvation, and deliverance. Nothing is impossible with Me.

My Child, you are blessed because you have Me, and because you are blessed, you have the responsibility to be a blessing to others. If you see someone down and dejected, lift them up with a smile and pour life into them. If you see hopelessness, bring hope. If you see sickness, bring healing. If there is a need, fill that need. When you do these things, you are a blessing. You are an extension of Me. You are My hand extended to the world. Now, go and be a BLESSING!

Love, God

Moments of Reflection

Date 11

Refined

The refining process is not enjoyable, but it is a necessary part of our Christian lives. What we want is to skip the refining part and go straight to the victory. Or maybe we just ask God to give us more of Him without allowing Him to refine and remove what shouldn't be in us. What we do not realize is; He'll never give you more until you can appreciate what you already have, and what you already have can become a foundation for more of Him.

However, we often lose ground with God and then expect Him to catapult us to a new level. Are you full of God and wanting more of Him? Or, are you full of the world and trying to put God on top of it all?

We cannot be full of the world and expect God to fill us up with more of Him. First, we must make room (repentance) for Him and then be filled up (Holy Ghost empowerment) with Him.

Romans 8:13, *"For if you live according to the flesh you will die; but if by the Spirit you put to death the deeds of the body, you will live."* (NIV)

Ephesians 4:25-32 *"Therefore, putting away lying, "Let each one of you speak truth with his neighbor,"[e] for we are members of one another. [26] "Be angry, and do not sin":[f] do not let the sun go down on your wrath, [27] nor give place to the devil. [28] Let him who stole steal no longer, but rather let him labor, working with his hands what is good, that he may have something to give him who has need. [29] Let no corrupt word proceed out of your mouth, but what is good for necessary edification, that it may impart grace to the hearers. [30] And do not grieve the Holy Spirit of God, by whom you were sealed for the day of redemption. [31] Let all bitterness, wrath, anger, clamor, and evil speaking be put away from you, with all malice. [32] And be kind to one another, tenderhearted, forgiving one another, even as God in Christ forgave you."*

So, it is crucial that we put off the things of this world and allow the Spirit of God to fill us. I've seen young Christians, try to put God on top of the sin that is in their lives. They didn't want to give up their sin; they wanted both, but it just doesn't work that way.

I Peter 1:15-16, *"But just as he who called you is holy, so be holy in all you do; [16] for it is written: "Be holy, because I am holy."* (NIV)

We must allow the refiner's fire to burn away the sin from our lives. As you spend time with God on this date, ask God to reveal sin or anything in your life that is not pleasing to Him. Allow Him to bring conviction and burn away the chaff.

I once asked the Holy Spirit to examine my heart and reveal to me anything that was displeasing to the Lord. I was surprised when conviction came. He revealed to me that I had allowed bitterness to come into my heart. He told me that I had a barrier up, and I would not be able to minister to other women unless I allowed Him to remove it. I remember denying it at first. Then, the sweet conviction of the Holy Spirit convinced me that it was true. I felt such a loving warmth from the Lord come over me. I wept and told God I was sorry, and I wanted Him to remove it. After many tears and much time in His presence, I began to feel the bitterness leave. I began to feel Him filling me with His love and Presence. I knew that He changed me that day because I allowed Him to work in me.

There are also times that we feel the prompting of the Holy Spirit to change or refresh an area in our lives. Sometimes this is an area we have tried to change in the past but failed. We feel conviction because we told the Lord we would change, but we never did. Then we feel like a failure when the Holy Spirit brings conviction again. We don't even want to think about trying because we think we will fail again. The devil has deceived us into believing this lie. So, we never change.

God is drawing you to Himself today. Ask yourself if you are willing to change the things God is revealing to you. As God brings conviction to your heart, remember it is because He has not given up on you and that He loves you enough to continue convicting your heart until you change. He does not see it as failure. He sees it as an opportunity to draw you closer to Him. He wants you to depend on Him for everything, especially for your faults and weaknesses. You may think, God wants YOU to be strong, but, HE actually wants to be strong in you. It is never too late to start again. No matter how many times you have failed in the past. Maybe this will be the time that you allow God to strengthen you and change you. But, you'll never know unless you start over again and let God be the strength in your life.

Daughter,

You are more precious to me than gold or silver. And all that I have can be yours. I hear you pray that you want more of Me, but that is not possible until you make room for Me. All through your life you have learned how to be strong and independent. By the world's standard that is a good thing. But, know that if you want to be strong, you must allow my strength to fill you up. I am your strength. Without me, you are weak. You need all that I have, to become all that I want you to be. I see so much potential in you. And, I love it when you lay down the things of this world and choose Me first.

My heart leaps when I see you changing into the woman of God that I created you to be. I have allowed you to make your own choices. And when you choose your own selfish desires, I don't stop loving you, I never will. I will give you chance after chance to choose Me first.

You are my precious possession, my treasure. There is no other person like you. You are my unique creation. When I look upon your face, I see the beauty of my creation. When I think of you, my heart is full. When I hear your voice say "Father, I love you," I am thrilled! When I created YOU, I said, "it is good."

My child, you have great things inside you that have been hidden just as treasures or gems are hidden, and they must be excavated or found to see their beauty. Some you know about, and some you haven't recognized yet. Don't allow the filth of this world to cover up the beauty that I have put inside you. I have placed gifts and spiritual gems in you. They are there for a purpose. I don't want them hidden any longer. I want to dig out some of those treasures. They are there for MY PURPOSE. They are there for MY GLORY. You were made for this reason, to SHINE for ME!
Love, God

Moments of Reflection

Date 12

Garment of Praise

My Story

A few years ago, my husband and I were in a state of hopelessness in our ministry. Nothing was going right, and we were even contemplating leaving our church. One Saturday night, we were at the church getting things ready for the service the next day. Neither one of us felt like being there. We were complaining about everything that was wrong at the church. We finally finished the mundane preparations, put on our coats, turned off the lights and started walking out of the sanctuary. Suddenly, I heard the Holy Spirit say, *"Praise Me."* It stopped me in my tracks. My husband said, *"Come on, what are you doing?"* I said to him, *"The Holy Spirit just told me to praise Him."* Then I turned the other direction and very quietly started saying *"I praise you, Lord."* Then the Holy Spirit said to me, *"Sing praises to Me."* So, I began singing quietly at first. I continued singing anything that came to mind.

I soon realized I was singing about things I was thankful for; then I got louder and louder. As I marched around the dark sanctuary singing, I began hearing my husband singing too. Now we were both marching around the sanctuary singing our praises to God. We thanked Him for any and everything we could think of, and when we couldn't think of anything else to praise Him for, we began singing in the spirit. We continued singing all the way home, and the next day, and for many days after that. We sang all the time, at home, in public, everywhere we sang. I remember trying to pray for people at the church, and all that would come out was singing. So, I began singing my prayers over people.

Before long, I began hearing people in our church singing praises to God. Walking down the halls and in the restrooms, you could hear singing all over the building. It was beautiful. This spirit of praise went on strong for a couple of months. I believe it broke hopelessness from my husband and me, and off our church.

In Isaiah 61:3 it says *to bestow on them a crown of beauty   instead of ashes,   the   oil of joy instead of mourning, and a garment of praise instead of a spirit of despair. They will be called oaks of righteousness,   a   planting of the LORD for   the display of his splendor.* (NIV)

The Hebrew root for garment is *atah*, which shows praise as more than a piece of clothing casually thrown over our shoulders. It quite literally means to wrap, cover, or envelop ourselves. The garment of praise is to leave no openings through which hostile elements can penetrate. This garment of praise repels and replaces the spirit of heaviness.

Have you ever felt hopeless about your life, ministry, health, family or other issues? If you want to get rid of hopelessness and despair, you must wrap or envelop yourself with the garment of praise. Then there will be no opening for the enemy to get in. When you envelope yourself in the garment of praise, you are creating a barrier that protects you from the enemy's devices. It's the secret weapon that the enemy doesn't want you to know about.

So, join me and begin praising God for everything you can think of. Begin your date with God by singing your praises to him. When we declare our love and praise for God with our voices, it breaks things in the spirit realm. Praise even and especially when you don't feel it. That is when it is most powerful! Soon, you will sense a breakthrough. When you sense a breakthrough coming, don't stop. Keep going. Continue praising and thanking God until you cannot think of anything else. Then pray and ask the Lord to bring to your remembrance prayers that He has answered and blessings and favor that have come your way. Believe me, if you ask God to help you remember, He will do it. He loves to be glorified for His greatness!

Another way I love to praise God is with dance. Like David, we should dance with all our might before the Lord. God loves it when we are willing to take our praise one step further and move our body for His Glory. Oh, How I love to dance, sing and praise my God! If you have not experienced this; it is time you start. I challenge you to put on some praise music and just go with it. Dance, and sing and praise with an unabashed love for your God. He deserves it.

Psalm 100:1-5 (NIV)

[1] Shout for joy to the Lord, all the earth.

[2] Worship the Lord with gladness;

come before him with joyful songs.

[3] Know that the Lord is God. It is he who made

us, and we are his[a]; we are his people,

the sheep of his pasture.

[4] Enter his gates with thanksgiving

and his courts with praise; give thanks

to him and praise his name.

[5] For the Lord is good and his love endures forever;

his faithfulness continues through all generations.

My Joy,

The hopelessness and void you feel in your life are not My will for you. When you allow hopelessness to take root, it will grow and choke the life out of you. It makes Me sad to see you struggling with these things. My will for you is to enjoy your life with freedom from these bondages. I want nothing more than to see you joyful and living in the promises I have given you.

I am the key to your joy. I am your hope. I am your freedom. Your victory will come when you step out in faith and praise Me. Allow Me to become your strength. Come away with Me and sing of My goodness. Sing about how you love Me. I love it when you praise me. If you want victory in your life, then begin by praising Me. Sing, shout and proclaim how I have saved you. Dance before me. Dance with all your might. Clap your hands and proclaim all I have done for you. Declare into the atmosphere my Holiness and my Power. I am the God that saves, heals, and delivers you.

Love,

Your Father

Moments of Reflection

Walking with God

God created Adam and Eve to walk in the garden with him. (Genesis 3) We were created to worship Him. That's why He loves it when we go to the secret place just to be with Him. Why is it we think that once we experience intimacy with Christ in the secret place, that we do not think we need to return to that place again? We need to walk in intimacy with Him every day. Even if we walk with Him every day, we still need to go to the secret place. We cannot live on our love from the past, but we need new refreshing experiences with God in the now.

God wants to walk with us and wants us to be one with Him. Christ is the Head, and we are the body. Col 2:19 says, *"and not holding fast to the Head, from whom all the body, nourished and knit together by joints and ligaments, grows with the increase that is from God."* We make up the many ligaments in the body.

Eph 4:3 says, *"— endeavoring to keep the unity of the Spirit in the bond of peace."* (KJV) Strong's meaning for bond: that which binds together, a band, bond of ligaments by which the members of the human body are united together that which is bound together, a bundle.

When the body is in unity, the ligaments work together to cause the body to go in a forward motion without hindrance. There are many ligaments in the body, but when they are in harmony, the body goes where the head tells it to go. When a ligament is injured, the body is slowed or stops altogether. The body is hindered from going forward and doing what it needs to do. No matter what the head tells it to do, the body cannot obey. The only way we can walk in unity with God is to be with Him.

Walking with God every day means being in unity with Him. When you move and flow with Him, it causes you to think and act differently. I have experienced both. I remember when I first came to this realization some years ago. I began to spend more time with the Lord, and it was evident that I began hearing Him more clearly. I remember while driving one day I heard the Holy Spirit tell me to go to a parking lot and minister to some ladies. I saw myself handing them a flower. So, I pulled over and went into a grocery store and bought some carnation flowers. I then drove to a parking lot and sat there praying. The Holy Spirit led me to six ladies that day. I will never forget that experience. As I walked toward those women, reaching out to hand them a flower, their guard came down immediately. Some of them smiled, and some cried and said thank you. I was able to pray with three ladies that day.

Thank God, I was obedient to the Lord's voice. I wonder how many times have I missed God's instruction because I was not walking in unity with Him and could not hear Him. My heart's desire is that you will begin to experience the same unity with God. Remember, you cannot walk with someone if they are not walking with you.

You have been going to the secret place for some time now, and you have learned that God wants us to experience His presence every day. Learning to hear from God daily and walking with Him every day is to have a relationship with Him. So, wherever we are, we can connect with Him and hear what He is saying to us. Then we can obey what He tells us to do. When we allow the head God to lead us, we find that we walk differently. We will go different places, and we will speak differently. As you go to God on this date, go with the realization that He created you to worship Him and be with Him. Make a point to connect with God every day this week. You will notice how your spiritual ears will be heightened to hear God more clearly. Learning how to move and flow with Him is a lifelong journey.

My Special Creation,
    Come and walk with Me and talk with Me daughter. I love it when we spend time together.

When you put away everything else and focus on Me, I know you will hear Me better. My desire is for you to become so familiar with My voice that you know it immediately. There are so many things I want to tell you. I have many plans for you. I have plans you could never dream of on your own. With me all things are possible. But, you must be able to hear me first.

As I begin to speak to you, be sure and respond to Me. I do not like to be ignored. When you hear Me give you instruction, respond with obedience. As you obey me more and more, I will trust you more and more. I have strategies and important missions I want you to hear and fulfill. As you obey, I will begin to trust you with important matters.

Don't depend on your own thoughts and feelings. They will only let you down. Know that you can be confident in what I speak to you. I will never go against My Word (the Bible). Now, seek Me, and when you do, you will find Me.

Love,

God

Moments of Reflection

Date 14

Pour In -Pour Out

Allow God to pour Himself into you today. There is so much that He has for you. He has an unmeasurable love that He wants to pour in. He has goodness and mercy ready to pour in. He has incredible power that He has given you if you will receive it.

God wants you to be filled up with His Spirit. His Spirit leads us from temptation, gives us discernment and gives us power to overcome the enemy.

Jesus was led by the Spirit. Luke 4:1 says, *"Then Jesus, being filled with the Holy Spirit, returned from the Jordan and was led by the Spirit into the wilderness."* When temptation came to Jesus in the wilderness, He was already filled with the Holy Spirit and was led by the Spirit. Jesus didn't stop and cry out to the Father to help Him. He didn't give up His fast and quit. He saw (thru the Spirit) that this was Satan tempting Him. His spirit rose up and took authority over His flesh. His flesh was weak, but because He was filled with the Spirit of God, He responded with the Spirit of Wisdom. Then He quoted the Word of God to Satan. We need to get the Word in us so that it comes out when it is needed. Be filled up every day. Then, when temptation comes, and the enemy comes in and tries to discourage you, you will be ready to fight it off by the POWER of the Holy Spirit that resides in you.

Jesus was full of faith because He had a daily, intimate relationship with His Father. He lived and ministered out of the overflow of His relationship with God. Because Jesus got the Word from the Father by the Holy Spirit, He could act upon it with clarity and understanding.

If we are filled up with the Spirit of God, then it is easy to hear God when He speaks.

When you allow the spirit of God to be poured into you, God expects you to pour it out onto someone else. Do you have something to pour? You can't pour out what you don't have. What are you pouring out to people--a refreshing drink or muddy stench? Are you ministering out of pain, anger, rejection, or fear? Or are you ministering out of a place of healing and victory? Pain happens, but when it does, we must take it to God, and allow Him to bring healing and victory to our lives. We can't afford not to go to the secret place. How can we minister to others if we haven't been ministered to ourselves first?

If you need strength or you have been hurt or rejected, come to the Father and allow Him to bring healing to your heart. God wants to pour into you His lifegiving Spirit today.

My Child,

My love for you has grown so much. I am so happy that you have set aside time to come and be in My presence. Stop for a moment. Close your eyes. Can you feel My breath in the wind? My Spirit is soaring around and through you even now. Do you feel My strength?

I am calling you to a higher place, a place you have only dreamed about. It is a place of freedom from your past hurts and fears. It's a place where only I AM. Do you want to go? You can. All you need do is TRUST ME. Know that I want to take you there. In this place, you will do mighty works for Me. All that you see yourself doing for Me is not just a dream. It can be a reality. I love to set people FREE and FILL them with My Presence and then USE them for MY GLORY. Daughter, you can be one of those people. I want that more than anything in the world for you. I created you for this purpose. When you SOAR, you are not alone; I am soaring with you. Make a covenant this day that you will not let anything hold you back any longer. Come, let Me be the strength in you. Then, we can FLY together.
Love,
Your Father

Moments of Reflection

Push

We all have push muscles in our arms. When we start working out to build them up, they become sore. However, if you continue working out, they get stronger and stronger.

When you push, it is to accomplish a goal. No one pushes for no reason. You push with all your strength to get a result. Pushing takes a lot of effort and includes your entire body at times.

When a woman gives birth, pushing can mean life or death. When I gave birth to my youngest son Craig, I remember pushing so hard; I thought I was dying. The Dr. kept telling me to push harder and I thought, *"I already am. There is nothing else in me that can push any harder."* The Dr. even had two nurses on each side of my abdomen pushing; trying to help me push my baby out.

Finally, the Dr. said Mrs. Burton, *"We are going to lose this baby if you don't push harder."* I'll never forget how that made me feel. I thought *I have no choice. Even if it kills me, I have to push harder.* So, I mustered all the strength I had and pushed harder than I thought I could, and out he came. The reward of seeing my baby alive was worth all the pushing I had to do.

For our spirit man to grow stronger, we need to push ourselves in our prayer time and the study of His Word. In fact, I've heard it said that the word PUSH could be used as an acronym for

P-ray
U-ntil
S-omething
H-appens

The apostle Paul stated in Philippians 3:14, *"I press on toward the goal to win the prize for which God has called me heavenward in Christ Jesus."* (NIV) We may think that we cannot go any further, but we can. We must push, push, push deeper into the things of God. We must Push forward in prayer; no matter what the circumstances.

To push through means to push into the secret place of intimacy with God. God is pleased with us when we seek Him, and therefore He rewards us. Hebrews 11:6 says, *"And without faith it is impossible to please God, because anyone who comes to him must believe that he exists and that he rewards those who earnestly seek him."* Paul says in 2 Timothy 4:8, *"Now there is in store for me the crown of righteousness, which the Lord, the righteous Judge, will award to me on that day—and not only to me but also to all who have longed for his appearing."* (NIV) God wants us to long for Him; He wants us to receive our heavenly reward. He has a crown of righteousness ready and waiting for us. Will you receive it?

This is your last date night using this book, but it certainly does not have to be the end of your secret rendezvous with Him. I am encouraging you to PUSH on. Do not stop having your special time with God. There is always more with Him. He will always take you higher than you were before. We never reach the end of the possibilities He has for us. So, keep going and PUSH in prayer, like your life depends on it. The rewards of pushing will be so worth it. Your reward will be your crown of righteousness.

My Child,

You have been spending much more time with Me, and that is wonderful. I have seen your heart of repentance, and I have witnessed your hunger for Me grow more and more. You are hearing Me clearer when I speak now, and I see my glory changing you, as you spend time with Me.

You now realize how valuable and altogether beautiful you are to Me. There is no other person like you. You are very precious to Me. I love you so much that I gave My Son's life so that you could have life.

You have also seen how My presence brings you rest and peace, in spite of the chaos that surrounds you. You have come to know the blessings of walking with Me every day, and you now know the importance of the secret place with Me.

The refining process has begun in you and will continue. Do not be afraid to let Me continue to burn away the things that are not like Me. For you to become more like Me, they must go.

Remember, My daughter, to love and cherish our time together because I do. Never let anything or anyone stop you from praising Me. I love it when you praise Me and thank Me for all I have done for you and for all that I am. Because I am God, the One, and only God.

So, don't give up on our time together. Don't allow distractions to get in the way of our relationship. Push past anything that tries to hinder you and push on toward your rewards. It will be worth it. I will be watching and waiting for you. I will be with you wherever you go. Day or night I am here. Remember our special times together in the secret place. I will be right here waiting for you!
Love,
Your God

Moments of Reflection

End Notes

Introduction
    1 "Secrets of the Secret Place" by Bob Sorge

Getting Started
    2 Eric Burtons's study on the five senses

Date 6
    2 Father's Love Letter used by permission,
Father Heart Communications ©1999
FathersLoveLetter.com

About the Author

Cynthia Burton is a credentialed minister with the Assemblies of God fellowship. She serves on the women's ministry cabinet at the Indiana District as well as assisting with the church planting assessments.

She and her husband Randall planted their church in Columbus, IN 23 years ago. Northview church has been experiencing an outpouring of God's presence since 2011.

Cynthia and Randall have traveled around the world igniting fires and aiding pastor's and their churches in going deeper into the things of God.

In her free time, she loves being with her family. She and Randall have been married for 35 years and have two sons and four granddaughters.

Please contact the Author at:
812-343-6450
2584 Lafayette Ave., Columbus, IN 47201
Email: secretarycin@sbcglobal.net